Compass

Winner of the 2013 T. S. Eliot Prize

The T. S. Eliot Prize for Poetry is an annual award sponsored by Truman State University Press for the best unpublished book-length collection of poetry in English, in honor of native Missourian T. S. Eliot's considerable intellectual and artistic legacy.

Judge for 2013: Sherod Santos

COMPASS
Luc Phinney

Truman State University Press
Kirksville, Missouri

Copyright © 2013 Truman State University Press, Kirksville, Missouri, 63501
All rights reserved
tsup.truman.edu

Cover art by Bob Phinney, *Hot Land*.

Cover design: Teresa Wheeler

Library of Congress Cataloging-in-Publication Data

Phinney, Luc.
[Poems. Selections]
Compass / Luc Phinney.
    pages cm. — (New Odyssey)
Poems.
ISBN 978-1-61248-096-1 (paperback : alk. paper)— ISBN 978-1-61248-097-8 (ebook)
I. Title.
PS3616.H49A6 2013
811'6—dc23

2013023571

To my wife and sons.

Contents

Part 3: The Work of the Echo

Acknowledgments

Descant: "Archaeologies of Knowledge," "After College"
Ecotone: "The Pleasures of the Alphabet," "A Dispensation from the Vows"
Hopkins Review: "Catoctin Lullaby"
Poetry East: "Compass"
Whole Terrain: "On the Way to Catoctin"

Part 1: The Work of the Hands

"Language is the house of being."
   —Martin Heidegger

"It is not necessary that buildings be beautiful, but it is necessary that they be necessary."
   —W. G. Clark

Archaeologies of Knowledge

I.

Under rusted aerials and drain elbows
and the alley cobbles, under downspouts'

buried cisterns and below the cool
hibernations of salamanders, past

newspaper-wrapped cached coin
and the plantain-soft lime left from some

unfinished plastering, below the glut
of conglomerate rocks, roadway aggregates,

below fragments of earthenware,
faceless majolicas, the iron of old roof nails

unspooling in the soil, below the sacked
bas-reliefs, scuffed tablets, vellum scraped clean

by microorganism in the slow drift
of continental shelf from the Atlantic

divergence to the micro-subduction of the Adrian,
and in all the crystalline dust rifted down

unfalling, I float, my feet at an atomic distance
from the floor, plumbed back in rough scumble

to some primeval father in the post-Hadean,
an archaeon consuming ocean, everything.

Above all things it is good to be alone
with the dark geometries of age.

II.

In a rift in the ground a cascade of arches
holds the earth jarred apart, and daylight

comes down from the street, down
past the sacristy of the basilica San Clemente,

where unfinished paintings hang, gathering
mildew's illuminations, down past the sussurus

of the afternoon tour, through the blur
and color of the stained mosaic floor, downstairs

to the first basement where the buried hall
of a medieval church suffers the occasional

scholar's flash, down and through the jointed stone
of that floor too, to the half-foundered walls

of a Roman house and its collapsed impluvium,
and down again through maidenhair ferns, mosses,

and over open-throated drains, to the lowest human plan,
one small Mithraic chamber where an altar rises

from the floor, under a curtain of noise that falls
continually from the high street, Colosseum traffic.

Somewhere above that white glare,
in the cabin of a Seven-Forty-Seven,

I cannot see, but feel,
the flecked pallor of my ex's face uncrease

as she leaves me in Rome, her lips
moving as she reads some scholarly article.

After College

Riding my bike to work in the dark before cars
flood the streets with their headlights,
I think a lot on molecules, cells
and vibration, what it is to be warm,
and what the nature is, of Being, in a freezing
universe, it's four o'clock and I'm the first one in.
I wet the tables, haul sacks of flour
through the open loading dock,
and clouds of steam light up
in miniscule dawn over the grey landscape
of the concrete floor, where I stand
in floured cotton, immense and groggy.

I watch the sky expand over the trees.
The oven smokes. I've burned
my priming batch, but I save
one loaf. Inside its dark-charred crust
the bread is moist. I eat a furtive breakfast,
leaning my head against the door's black glass.

Thrownness

In the dark barn on a wheel
slip spins in a whorl, a curl of clay
left underneath the finished vessel.

I listen to the rain drive down,
and to the tin roof drum,
an unceasing stumble. I throw

another vase, a mixing bowl, and then
an odd-mouthed urn,
clay pressing on cupped hands,

stilling its uncertain motion
in my own. Low, beneath the rain,
I hear the motor's drone

and buzz, and feel the accustomed force
pressing the clay against
my hands, and yet I've never

brought the casing off,
or looked inside, to see if cord
and motor come together

in a clip, a wire-nut, some form
of grammar. The wheel spins,
allowing me to work within

the grammar of the form,
plumb to the vessel's lines, its fall
toward something only ever somewhat

final. Meanwhile the rain keeps
trailing down, folding
and unfolding the mountains, finding

clay and silt in thin soil
and washing it out
to curl in the river, to cloud

the water with clouds'
cumbrous roil, doubling and dividing,
turning over itself releasing

itself subsuming the man, absolving him
of the erratic drip of the p-trap
under the kitchen

countertop, of the chipped
dishes in the sink crusted
with last night's dinner,

of hands, chapped except
where they are pruned, plunged
to the elbow in, this time

a cylinder, this time a cup,
a pot, a plate, a bottle
warmer, something somehow

of some use, some permanence.
Surely, at last, back in the house,
the infant must be sleeping,

holding in himself, in the tumult
of his blood, his breathless
wail. Meanwhile,

in the roar and thunder, I look up
bewildered from this motion
as the sun, somehow come

round into the clouds'
endings, opens them
into a formless form.

Compass

One morning at the lake's edge
you find the rocks arranged
in a compass shape,
some stacked in cairns,
some dropped akimbo,
some crossing, some ringing
the cross. You love it, and are angry
all at once. Who was here?
What thief of privacy loves
art, and leaves notes?

The air flows over the lake
and is, as usual, blank,
white, waiting
for the ringing marks
of hammer and nails
(three cents a pound).
The cabin is more
than an idea, less than a thing,
and the leaves' notes fall over it,
an inordinate music.

Robinson

I lift a beam on my ad-hoc block and tackle,
lash it off, shimmy down one stripped bole
and go across and up the other post

to the beam's butt-end, climbing
to the level of the deck, or what will be
the deck of my tree house, when it is finished.

I'm high up, and the wind
rises then, lifting the sweat off my back
and making my knees weak, a brief

flight. Then, balanced, I cinch down
a half-hitch and the first
crosspiece is fast. I look out across

the treetops to the beach, where the wrack
of my ship beats, still heaving on the reef.
It has been a week and still the wreck bucks,

groaning against the impregnable
rocks. I've lost Milton, Shakespeare, Donne,
their spines undone by tidal bore and purse.

I'm down to only those few words
the mind contains, and those multitudes
it can. I mutter them, call, chatter, caterwaul,

anything to make the ceaseless rushing
trees and tides a bit less inhumane.
The trades swallow everything.

I hear music all the time: tide pushing
through a tube of rock, sighing and spouting.
Birds drunk on rotted fruit. The snap

of canvas overhead. Dusk, and the litter
of bats' sonar. Rainwater on leaves, on cloth,
on the wood deck of my half-finished house,

water on water, water soaking into soil, water sheeting
off rocks, boiling and coursing as on a ship's deck in storm.
Landfall made, the land will stop its heaving soon, I know

from past experience. This music has more permanence.
Often I return from being lost in sounds,
to find I'm lost again: the horizon gleaming

with its usual fire, chop on the deep diminishing,
averaging with distance, dark beneath its cover
of reflected gold. It is true of distance, that it remains

abstract: unbroken by a single second's tick, minutes
summing to degrees, degrees compassing
all sea and sky, despite the eyes'

occasional flaws, which I read as gnats
or fleets or masts of brailed ships, a flare
of hope, and cold. The wind, struck dumb

momentarily, returns louder and more strange
and I'm remembered to my lostness, returned
to solitude, salt cod, bananas.

God, when I said I wanted never
to hear another angry voice again,
surely you recognized the hyperbole.

So many days the sunset wakes me
to the work I've done,
and I return to being

all at once alone. So many days'
unchanging change, the project I had thought
to be a matter of some months

grown now to years and still unfinished;
I doubt completion; I cease to care; my hands
somehow are stained and thick and sore,

but pleasantly. I feel the strength in them,
the youth spent from them, spent for something
only mostly square, a structure part lean-to and part aerie

and part air, which I will leave without hesitation.
Whether returned at last to my lost home,
or tumbled from my high solitary blind,

(nothing but sky above me and around me and the wind
gone quiet, being subsumed itself in wind,
and the understanding I am falling coming only as the ground

strikes me back into a windless body,
lying in the duff, still feeling falling
as I watch the clouds unfurl in semaphore).

I know what I have come to know
only after all this building:
though I am salvaged, I will not be saved.

God, when I promised to Believe
if you brought me through that storm to land,
I believed I would believe,

but couldn't comprehend
the reach of the wild, in which I'm ever
animal, miniscule, except that time I am aloft—

then, uncoupled from this earth
the land below becomes an Eden
I am Adam to, perfectible,

unmoored, unmanned. Loving it,
I delay returning to the ground
as long as I can.

In storm, curtains of rain
blow into the room. There is no light on them
but there is light in them. The house

rocks, but does not heave. It is no ship.
It is only the house I will have left
if you read this.

Apsis

Sparks spray.
 My angle grinder
cuts through a fence post base.
Faces lit, boys crowd
the caution tape,
their play momentarily
lapsed. I stand, arch
my back.

I set the grinder down,
 sit on a nearby stone. I touch
numbers. 1814. 1810.
 A name.
Numbers again.
Another name:
a family plot. The boys
at play go back to throwing sand,
 waiting for their parents
to come. To pick them up. To reclaim them

from the churchyard.
Why has it been so long?
They want to walk
 like grown-ups, run
like horses. They feel their legs,
like phantom limbs, still move.

They wait—
 for God
to rapture them?
 for cloning?
for perfect rendition in art?
Or just a quick rubbing?

Sun glints in the lapis glass
    in the apse
        beyond this potters' field
where stones rise,
on the roots of bluegrass
frost heaves
the moon's mass—

God Speaks

GOD Speketh:
I perceyve here in my majestye
How that all creatures be to me unkynde,
Lyvynge without drede in worldely prosperytye;
Of ghostly syght the people be so blynde.
—*Everyman*, Act 1, Scene II

Man, even before the Flood
you'd already given up
on a methodical approach to beauty.

Was it Eve,
in her matchless summer dress?
Or lichen crusting a boulder

in the grassy field where she ran,
and you pursued?
Or was it panicles

of yarrow in the sun,
switchgrass, insects,
the play of rain and gold?

Man, what work is this?
One of us sits still,
watching in the dark,

for trespassers? Not me!
I'm down between the aisles
of stacked wrecked cars,

walking over broken windshield
glass, crushed gravel, the fallen
mitten leaves of sassafras,

brushing a hand across
the efflorescences of rust,
swirling the puddled oils,

counting the myriad
teeth of mice adjacent to a fragment
of Mark Twain, numbering again

the sum of everything
abandoned to rot
and rain, my brassy

dream song dumb with quantum
inattention. Lit blue,
your gate shed draws bugs, flickers,

flares, saccades with the lightwash
of car chases, old flames, torch
singers—but those fires

aren't bright enough
to moth me. You? But wait—
is someone out there in the dark?

Man, you're still night-blind
but that should change—
Look up, through the tracks of branches,

through the cumbrous cloud,
listen to the zapper's
chatter and the thud

of hip-hop from a party
down the road, thunder
made small. I call

into the quiet like a fulvous owl.
Come out! Your flashlight raises
dust to meaning. I breathe

and you think: Ghost —God—ferric
dust from someone's
totaled ride. Who?

No one. But look here, man,
now that we're alone—
isn't that a redbud

in bloom, growing
through the hurricane
fence? Listen, do you hear it now?

The hum and flit and quiver,
the blues of the bees collecting
endless nectar?

At the Forge after an Argument

At last the coal inside my head has all
burned down to coke, and I am cancellous,
soot-black, I am intemperate. The skin
of my head pulses as I hammer out
an umber bar, the clangor injuring
the ear and freeing it from indenture.
I have only the one iron in this fire,
and heat pours into it until it glows
past white, spits sparks, and sublimates, lit motes
rising and starring the barn's dark-mattered air.
I carry on until what's left is slewed
past useful form, a curl of steel seeming
to grasp for what I cannot ever have
again: the blacksmith's blank, wife-bodied soft.

Residences

1. Fall

Let me live without constraint,
too rich for rent, too poor for money
management, let me go to a lake house
not for one occasional weekend but for all
the fall's long days, when the low light plies
the colored wake of maples. Give me worthwhile work
while there—a deck begun under green shade
to be completed in the discovery of sun
where it has not been for months, the understory
and the framing overhead rippled
with waterlight, shifting persimmon,
paramecium, shadow coming
and going, something of the wet and something
of the sun tracing their interference patterns.
Let me drink clear water on the new deck's height,
and cold black beer as night's weight
falls over the lake.
May it erase all my work, for forgetting
is lovely at night. Let me wake early
and go out to fit handrails, coffee steaming
in its stainless thermos, the deck slick
with a matte frost, let me skate
across that surface, allow me to glide to a stop
before the unguarded edge, arms out windmilling.

May the carburetor in my '79 Camino
not plug up, and preserve
the running boards from rust. Flood
the cab with Baptist preacher radio,
or banjo blues, and let it all come through

without unusual clarity, that the hiss and pop
may overlay old songs, something like the arias
of UFOs. Preserve me though
from all abductions and probings, I'm too young
for cynicism, too old to fully heal.

2. Winter

Let me go up to a penthouse suite
where the snow is spread out smooth and demarcates
a new map of the city's diesel-crusted streets.
Give me Grohe or Hansgrohe trim to run my hand,
satin, along, and other proper work, not anything
involving the computer, let me hang big sheets
of white Sheetrock—not 4 x 8, but 4 x 12—
and paint them with a mural's narrative debauchery
in white-on-white, but before I do, allow
the screw-gun's whine to sing its descant
endlessly, make my hands ductile with youth
and adroit from long practice
with trowels, towels, and the spoils
of hubbub and minimal speech in late-night bars,
where I can be, surely, anonymous, seeing X-ray–style
through walls of various transparencies, to the iron traceries
of roof drains and the various nonferrous metals
electric with voice and the ephemeral gesture.
Forgive me, too, for telling the girl I loved her
purely for sex. Anemone. Moon jelly.

When I need the next paycheck
before it comes, let there be a payday-loans
nearby, and may no casino share its strip-mall strip,
and if it does allow the slots to be liberal,
more so even than the public radio.

3. Spring

Allow me both the wealth
to build a butterfly-roofed cabin
on a bluff of sandy soil by the river,
and free time to spend there where the aspen
parse the slow erosions of the wind, sufficient time
to stay for the sudden change spring calls
into the land, the willows' millions
coloring, a flood of salmon,
chartreuse, viridian. Give me the grace
to set my roto-hammer down, and go out
to walk along the fishing access trail,
and may the ticks still sleep while all the grasses
rise and bloom. Give me sure feet
where spring flood cuts the old path through,
and may the muskrat cast his stink
on someone else's dog. Let me spend
my best days in the shade, trenching culvert
underneath the road.

On Sundays let me be somewhere remote,
far from the madder red of this or that illuminated God,
encyclic, anthropic—instead,
give me something fluid, some sermonette,
a quick cascade of freshet over rocks,
and may the leaches near my blood-numb feet
remain encysted, summer having not come yet
to light the beargrass in this unnamed draw.

4. Summer

Let me walk beneath the ginkgo
and the goldenrain tree, where the little pale
bodies of the tulips sleep their summer sleep
beneath bluegrass, fescues, and the nets of the subsurface
irrigation pipes, amid the redwoods' roots,

and the serpentine roads worms make
in their multitudes, beside a white-towered
Victorian house all frilly with old gingerbread,
and may the scaffolding present me
solidly to that façade.
Give me rhubarb, wide as a winged
serpent, give me foxglove irising in rain,
give me lovemaking with a dryad
in an alder grove, let me never
go inside again. Let every house I build
hold its windows open
to the wind, and give me many
second homes, none of them to own.

I'm no spark plug, but I know
my arms bleed strength, and atrophy
with every pleasure. Forget pleasure.
Let me hang unlit light-strings
in the trees, give me a plastic chair
to sit myself down in, and let the roof deck
lift me up in sundown's sun, give me
the only work that matters:
let me walk in beauty, climb ladders.

Ars Poetica

The rain stops and you take him out to play in the garden.
You weed. He whacks the raspberries. The rain begins again.

You take him to the attic, then to the basement.
He kicks over stacks of books waiting to be shelved.

There is blackness all around you. The sun, the sun.
He has gone to dig under the fir tree in the yard.

He throws cones and needles everywhere.
The sky is a whorl of blue.

In the time it takes you to write this
he has built a city, acropolis and all.

Over it tufts of cottonwood parasail,
gliding through shafts of light and shade.

He wanders over to check on you.
He hands you his shovel. It's a trade, see? For the pen.

Part 2: The Work of the Song

ποταμοῖσι τοῖσιν αὐτοῖσιν ἐμβαίνουσιν, ἕτερα καὶ ἕτερα ὕδατα ἐπιρρεῖ.
"Each time we step into the same river, different waters overflow us."
　　　　—Heraclitus

Market Closing

Peppers hang in chains over the clutter in the street.
Crowds ebbed, it clouds, and rains; gulls dive for flawed fruit.

The sun flares below cumulus, and a woman lights
the wick of her shadow. The wind's flights

chill her, sieve her. Still, ahead of her the litter
is a sea. She walks on, lost in sun and brailed all over

with the cold's friction. Woman of secret skin, I aim
to take the private language of your arm,

and kick through cast-off flowers. In sum:
to walk you home.

Turnings of Fire

Sheets are often like a glacier.
Oftener they're like a river.
Slick with the night's silver,

the delta water rises quiet;
crests curl, touching cold.
Shadows play in stream, lifting up

the fish of her limbs, the rocks of her bones,
a heat of laughter unreleased
from chest or halter, a drifter,

lifter, levitator. In this water
she is ever other, first lover,
first of the turnings of fire.

Sub Rosa

In the dark of her room
in early winter I become the man
who raped her. She shrinks
into the wall's corner, slatted
with the blinds' stripes; she pulls
the blanket around herself. Soon,
I think, it will be too late in the year
to leave the window open while we sleep.
She cries carefully. In the window
the streetlight sketches circles in the persimmon,
and I trace them: *Diospyros*
virginiana, the native persimmon, more delicate
in its branchwork and smaller of fruit
than the cultivated variety, *Diospyros kaki*,
often seen in stir-fry, or simply
eaten hand-to-mouth, like an apple
but less sweet, peppery like a desert
apricot, bitter, in part, as a pomegranate's
white integument—*Punica granatum*, that—
and not unlike the pith of citrus fruits—
All this time she is shaking
fetal facing the wall unable
to put words to what has changed,
but I can guess, this isn't the first time
I've been ghosted by some sick
bastard of a man—stranger?
teacher? friend?—and listened,
lost, to the wind press
on the window glass.
Over the persimmon in the alley some crows turn,
and over them the radial array of the city's heat
rises up, cooling and blending

as it lifts through layers of uncondensed
cloud, lost falls, radio noise,
and rising, passes out into the soundless cold
where contrails seem to, but do not, cross.
I rest my hand on her arm, then trace
one shoulder blade. "I'm here," I want to say, but find
I can't. After some time I take my hand back.

On Visiting a Brutalist Monastery near Éveux, France

Couvent de la Tourette, Charles-
Edouard Jeanneret-Gris (Le
Corbusier), 1957–60

1.

The glass of her dress was a red glass
and she, no figurine, glowed in the failing
evening, her rough skin made soft
in the saturation of that light, a light
so rich it smoothed even the *couvent*'s
gunnite skin, and made us
intimate, who had come
in separate tour groups.

2.

Strangers still, we came into the door
of the day's end and stood in it together
and kissed there like old lovers,
with a passion part willed and part
remembered, there at the foot of that cliff,
that berg, that beached tanker-hull,
the dye of her dress
bleeding in the red sun's wash and fall.

3.

The wind was flowing in the grass
as we walked through the monastery trees,
espying the espalier, and pocketing

fruit, beside light wells so hot with the sunset
they kilned us in the field, her cheeks blood-flushed
and clouded-about with gnats, the buzzing whine
gone slow, Gregorian, sunk now
below human hearing.

4.

Coming late into the unlit
chapel after everyone had gone, we ran
our hands beneath the math of modern
tapestries, over the hidden compass
of the concrete walls, lost
in the language of sand and aggregates
and made small together
in the vault of the mouth.

Slough

Walking the bank of the slough, I plumb
your gone self and skin, your vocalism
censored by the main
motion of the thing, turn of the armillaried
world, ellipsoid corkscrew, the path
runs so straight through it must be
unavoidable, must be enough. I press
through overgrown broom, raise stellar
nurseries of pollen, press on, the lath
of leaves and sticks passing me piece
by piece, each day a weft
for the warp of my life left.

Down the unlit channel,
down through the city's arroyo
and clough this dark band bends,
a breathless breath a sheaf a cloth
a band of black uncertain stuff
an origin to both of us, then one—
One starred, fired, stray, spun
on under pinwheeling constellations,
blundering among the seedheads
of grasses, loosestrife,
sloughing off the chaff of company.

On the water in the night
the moon hops from trough to trough,
scattering itself.

Contemplating Proposing

In the blue overhead
there are birds,
the stained park bench
creaks as I move,
and again as she moves,
and there is something
of the ocean in the blood's
occupation of the ears.

Overhead, faintly sweet,
the locust blooms, tiny
pea-shaped men
parachuting down
to crawl the beaches
of her collarbones.

Wedding Night
in a Tipi

I woke in a space
culled from the grassy field,
the earth beneath me
slipping forward.

The night just past, already lost,
dispersed—flushed skylit
cone, fire guttering to gray
beside the cindered Pendletons.

Over us the tipi
broke from its Salish dream.
I slipped from sleep to dawn
and watched her surfacing,

the henna of her skin
paling with morning,
flat grass rising next to her
in my body-trough.

Hidden Lake

48.663559, –113.750002, Glacier, Montana

Did the mountain goat who followed
my wife in her wedding dress

wonder how the beargrass had evolved
to lace, or contemplate the chase,

or think, is this the sun-behind-the-cloud
of sensual delight at last embodied? I watched him pace

with measured tread, an even ten feet at her back
and thought, "Oh shit—we're on *When Wild Animals Attack!*"

Early Ultrasound

"Jellyfish have existed in the seas of the earth for 650 million years and will probably continue to exist as long as there are seas."
—Suzanne Tate

If lungs could swim from the slough of ribs and float in air, serene, primordial; if luff of skin moved in a slowness agate-orange, lit from within; if corpuscle and the cilial strake of artery borrowed peony speech, blush of hybrid and infallible rose; if the mind itself in all its cellulose, wrapped like an onion around the child, could be loosed and set adrift, trailing streamer through the garden of high atmosphere; if sky turned cannibal to sky amid the failing light following vulcanism; if blue bottle, jimble box, banded jelly, winged comb jelly, black sea nettle, crystal jelly, paper lantern, lion's mane, sea wasp, fragile comb, lucent jelly, moon jelly; then— surely—son.

At 9 Months

There are no faces on those little rock carvings,
hips and breasts geologic, massy. Here, too, the water
that eases the edges of rocks everywhere
has made this woman round, though in the scrim
of steam behind the vinyl shower curtain
her voice is low and rough, her darkened nipples clear.

Kairos Being Born

καιρός: *a significant moment; weather;*
indeterminate or non-chronological time.

Each of the dots of water comes whole
into the world from the chrome showerhead.
Falling on rock walls of imitation
travertine, rucked cloth, and skin, they purl down
and join together in the drain, taking on
the shape of sewer lines, root-crowns,
the Amazon, of lightning-in-rain, cities
seen from planes, veins lining
lips pressed, spread of wet hair tangled
on her neck, birth pain, nerve tracks.

In the shower in the hospital
my wife labors in my arms, her skin
gone rigid and then slack and soft,
and she is wet and mostly naked under
the lukewarm spray and I
am mostly naked too and we
slump in the endless water falling, water
beading on her shoulder blades
in an unending flood
of what must be rain.

Being man, I can only hold her
in this stream and rock and hum in human
confusion, lost in the cosmos
of closed eyes, of William
Kairos being born.

A Father's Vertigo

It's been two nights and still my wife and son
have not come home—she six (and some) pounds less
and he, too small to seem wholly human
in goggles under bilirubin lights.
I knock around the house, and file down burrs
on banisters, whitewash the stoop, and sit
with doors propped open to the evening breeze,
the nursery off-gassing fresh-paint scent.
I'm father to something I can't visit,
can't even name without feeling some doubt.
I listen to the crickets, dry and faint;
and what I feel and should feel remain separate.
I'm half giddy, half sick—though one assumes
singular causes: fatherhood: paint fumes.

The Circumcision

I hold his tiny hands as he cries.
Later, I will help him into his saffron robe
and snap the two small snaps.

He balls his fists
in my fists. I can feel sweat
rise on my skin in sympathy with his. I look

into his face to try to see his adult face.
I look into the window's shadow
of myself. Beyond, beside the half-flooded

Clark Fork, under the leaning
cottonwoods, a backhoe diesels in the shade.
I wonder—Is it safe to be so red?

So angry? So scared? And if the glans,
presumably unharmed, should still exude
the tiny droplets of his blood?

I make myself look on, witness
the wad of epidermis cut away
and crumpled to the side.

When this is over I will take him
back to the half-completed house,
and abandon him to sleep.

Of Apples and Architects

He knows how much she needed
this: to go out from the roadside lot
into the apple trees to pick
the apples by herself. She made it
clear; the infant
cries without her.

He wants to be back
at work, and hates
wanting to be anywhere but here,
and draws doodles
in the air, his fingers
desperate and wiggly. The child
cries, his noise rising
over the road dust, crows, flies,
the flaws in the orchard's
methodical quinqunx, places
the tongue moves over.

Holes; hedgerows, blackhaw, hawthorne,
fall apples held concealed
under leaves; how curves
are always hard to make
with modular materials; how structures
camber under the unlikely loads;
how many e-mails has he had, unread.

He feels resentment burning
in his skin, imagines his wife
moving her hands under the leaves
amid the apples, he desires her

again, it moves in him,
and damn it surely she can hear
the child as it cries
and cries while she says gone.
Surely the tantrum is carried
in the wind. Surely this will
end; but it goes on.

He leans his head against the doorframe
of the car, and stares down
at his crying son.
He will have been so happy.

Aubade, with Legos

Last night I wiped projectile vomit
off the back seat of our new Honda,
(the one we rationalized we could afford)

and we drove home too late, the kids crying
and muttering themselves to sleep
in an acrid and piney funk.

This morning the heat is broken
and you curl with infant and older son,
still sleeping under layers of covers,

while I go get the coffee on, hoping
the oil has run out,
and this is nothing I can fix.

I've cranked the space heaters up
as far as they can go, and when I jump
back into bed I land on Legos; feel

your skin, humid from the shower; listen
to the window frames wrack under
the pressure of the wind. Was it Racine

who said that pleasure is the absence
of pain? The old down comforter is a baffled
scudding cloud, and we are birds

aloft in it, or rain, we are passing high
over some snow-blanketed plain
dotted with immaculate blocks of houses.

A Night in the Hospital

In that endless time when you are crying
with an utter clotted desolation and I'm holding you
in that one position which seems to ease you away
from gagging, aspirating, filling small
lungs gone pneumonial, I slip from my body,
dizzy, a spiral school of smelt or shad, something
numerous and small, I'm watching you judder
in my arms and I'm too ocean-gone
to feel you move, the world rises and falls
and the room writhes with plankton,
which I know must be nothing, surely,
just a glitch in the vitreous fluid of my cornea.

Escapement

My son has woken up and I can hear,
faint, beyond the vacuum in the walls,
his small voice counting down, or up, or else
his damped cadence is a nonsense-song,
a thing he's stolen from the intimate
math and moonscape of his starry sleep,
something of the mainspring of the world
in which his dad, downstairs, hears only slippages.

Now he comes downstairs, and the sound of him
is less, and more, than the sound of feet, and I listen
to the quiet that falls between footfalls.
"Hey dad," he says, "do you know what moondogs drink
for midnight snack?" I pour the Milky Way into his glass
somewhere under the vast night's cataract.

Catoctin Lullaby

Boys, it's time for bed. I know
you loved this day so much,
and that it was, of all grey days

a perfect grey day,
that there were so many
circuits of the sky,

while sun still lit the candles
in the woods, still made
song of the uncertain rain.

You're sleeping now. I listen to the frogs
voicing their cry in short pips
that sum to one continuous rise of sound

that just keeps rising, if it were light
or if we saw in sound like bats
or dolphins do, as light it would seem

like rain falling up, and like rain
circling the surface of a pond,
all at once and everywhere,

a phosphorescent wake of some
omnipresent whalesong, trailing
through the branched wrack

of the understory, inordinate
and bright, the flooding
of a sound still rising up, still roiling,

still ringing and uncurling, netting,
diffracting, outlining
the soft breathing of each tree,

each bouldered ridge, each arch
of elm and beech, rimed
not in moonlight but in the hum

and churr of a night overrun
with frogs, organism
underneath this dream, the dream,

boys, I'm sending you over draws
coursed with streams and rivulets
and flocked with the shadow

of the failing hemlocks, over
the soft rock faces hidden
under hickory and oak, over cabins

in meadows and the matte patchwork
of farmers' fields. I'm sending this lit night
into the city, where it will blend

into the traffic of the rain
and find some route to your
indistinct room, Plum Street, Oak Street,

Hophornbeam, and wait there
in the ceiling's fraying corners
till you wake, fitful, from a dream

of blue-green waves, of lighting
bugs, of your dad, indistinct
in the woods, and then the light of this

lost place will sift down, sough down,
and find the shadows in your room,
and fill them, that you may know

I am here in these woods,
in just such a dark
as yours. Boys, I know I am not home

to chase you to bed, or come
quietly upstairs to check
the sweet freedom of your sleep.

I know nothing will remain of this
in memory but that we were without
each other, stripped of lullaby

and story, separate
in whatever glory the world
perpetually lets fall. My boys,

I know I have less time than I had thought
for you to be too young to remember
your dad gone from home.

Propagations
of Days

1.

Last night the weight of sleep
came down on me
and everything went black—
not everything that I could see
or feel alone but everything
I was. It was no different
from being dead, except, post-infinite,
I would begin again, confused,
amoebic, having budded
off from my own end,
leaving again the dark, alone,
to the harness of its tides.

2.

Between the tough-love narratives,
the morning lists, emails, flash-chats,
cold calls, I sit down at the formica
breakfast bar and roll ham into rolls
in taco shells, and pack them up
in each lunch sack. In the image
photo-printed on the counter top
the fossil shells of ammonites cluster
and circulate, tracing out whatever
currents brought them to this point,
whatever routes or fonts of nutrients
called them, and gave them to swim
together in such profligate daylight,
in the loose rain of diatoms, even
as they were laid into the rock.

Bedtime

I tell the boys another jungle story
to quiet them, as they are drifting off.
That's it. That's all. I have no more. I'm sorry.

Cheetah and Monkey find an old dune buggy
and travel to the edge of Beeny cliff.
I tell the boys another jungle story.

One starts to cry. I listen to his body
clutch and flail. The other starts to cough.
That's it. That's all. I have no more. I'm sorry.

Now both are crying and I want to bury
my head in my armpit like a giant sloth.
I tell the boys another jungle story.

Dolphins sport over the phosphorescent algae.
The animals all sleep out on the reef.
That's it. That's all. I have no more. I'm sorry.

In the quiet room I listen to the fury
of my pulse slow down. I know it will be brief.
I tell the boys another jungle story.
That's it. That's all. I have no more. I'm sorry.

Part 3: The Work of the Echo

"I could be bounded in …
                         … infinite space."
        —*Hamlet,* Act 2, Scene 2

Midnight
at the Cabin

The wind pushes the door open
and comes into the room,
the doorway holding something other
than the blueblack lake.

I struggle up from sleep
too late, hearing the distant
running of the rain.

Dispatch

The car in the inner lane hit the bike messenger
after a family van had stopped, and waved him on.
She listened.
He had time, before he died,
to watch clouds tumble in the steel-blue sky.
In the weeks that followed
she would wake in the quick of her rage.
It was a gust, a grunt, less than a name.
"This is dispatch," she said, "please repeat."

Cabbage Moths

1. Bayard Phinney 1914–1988

Theirs is a kamikazi-ing randomness,
            a flaring of chaff, a falling
     and diving through air
                  strafed with the early
       apricot's flower.
How they are wild to avoid my net!
         But, willful or not,
     they are bound to the brassicas,
forced by the weight of their eggs
         which burn to unfurl
    in lazy and ravenous fire
as the broccoli mature.
       Later in summer
I'll kick the flawed
heads apart.

2. Viola Phinney 1919–2005

I watch him out the kitchen window,
my husband of so many years,
sweeping his net through the air,
his face creased in his hat's shadow.
When the net bites, his face clears,
drops age, and is the face of the soldier
I waited for. I know what waiting is
the way this window opens to the winds.

Soon he is raising a ruckus again,
swishing his net like he's fishing,
englobed by the cabbage moths, sun-
lit, light on his feet, his eyes flashing.
They are so improbably pure,
as if hundreds of dresses   were falling through air.

The Call

for Ariel

Before color has come back into the ball fields, before the cloud lid on the valley
    lifts, before sound
from her phone's small speaker passes down the cochlear passage and is transformed
to meaning in the brain, the wind blows through her red hair, spreading it out into
    the grass
which is, after all, suddenly green. She is in her body the way a bird is in the sky,
her dress is too light for the cold day, there is sand in her shoes from the sandbox
    at work,
but it is also sand from a beach far away and long ago, and she is altogether
other, Precambrian, serene, and the black shapes reeling over her
are something prior to birds, prior to the numb club
of her too-human hand which has been holding the phone
all this time, as one by one the words come to her
lying on the ground, and she hears
her mother's gone.

Inchoate

"You can miss the most important years of
your life, the years of possible creation."
—John Coltrane

If Coltrane is a river or a rain
of notes, radio static must be earth
itself, fertile and undifferentiated, blackbody

white noise, the chittering of stars in space and the long
journey of light in space, summed. You hear
she won't be coming back, the woman

who worked a few desks down,
her 672nd Engineers caught forward
somewhere, and something else, you hear backchatter

on the line, Mandarin or Farsi, a meaningless grafitti.
It is early spring where you are; it must be early
spring everywhere and the one

river is gravid, grey with silt. A sign—a plasma-cut
trout, gunmetal blue—swings and is still, and over it
apartment windows *oh*, one or two

half-open, forming words of exhalation, you listen
to static, wait for meaning to descend, you want
to write it all down but the clouds hang,

and drift, and won't combine. Waiting at a light
a jogger hops in place on the sidewalk, her legs nubbled
with gooseflesh. Her earbuds carry her in an unbridgeable

privacy, you will never know her song, but you can see
the evidence of song in the rhythm of her. The river
rises and the clouds come down from blinding

sky and the music, when at last you hear it, is sweet.
Jot quick! Tap feet! Mutter,
scribble on paper. Get it down. The pattern

will come, trust it will come.
There's little else to go on.

Circuit

I.

In old age will I dream
and dream of snow? If bee,
somehow assume god-
particle? If shoal
then open-netted rocks,
rocks open as fish
shoaling gathered
loose in vast
recurring ciphers,
motions seeming
random only
individually nonsensical?
In unceasing
motions, school of clouddrift,
of pollencount, of windweft
and windwarp, in
the new burl
and knot and streaming-out
of one bee's
telling of one
path, one route,
the net of hive and flower
and rotting fruit and sweet
popsicle-melt, fruit-floe,
honeydew rind, hummingbird
feeder, chorizo, pure
tomato katsup slopped
from little packets,
and hovering in its
completed circuit one
bee starting up its storytelling,

buzzing, snoring, shaking,
dream-dancing in its mystical
communion, Ouija-motion, telling
everything in the world
in one string,
one naming made
one-way, one note
samba, scent-shape, lacking-sweet,
elsewhere-other-nectar-follow-me—

Larkin's Blue Wonder

"There is nothing quite like the argot of the artificial fly. What other sport could offer the Shaving Brush, Sassy Cat, Rich Widow, Mormon Girl, Silver Fairy, Wickham's Blind Fancy or December Gold?"
— Steve Raymond, *Rivers of the Heart: A Fly-Fishing Memoir*

I'm flying, again, my body as light
as it ever was, when I was young
and made for this. Now, I'm reconstructed,
curvaceous, pure of heart or without
heart, I'm not sure. No matter. Among
the rampant gold of grass heads I'm dead
only on paper, each resurrection feels
as real as puncturing hooks, nails.

My flight's curtailed, not lazy anymore,
jerking over the same stretch of water.
It's beautiful here. Each river is pure,
and I tell myself I chose this, foreswore
adventure and aubade, made pleasure
second to what I could know for sure.
Of course I miss the rest of my corps,
and dread the tackle box, and my drawer.

I'm a study of artifice. I have, in place
of my old wings, foam fakes.
Pthalo blue, my thorax glitters
with automotive paint, my face
mounts two great Quik-Affix
eyes, my antenna are radio transmitters.
I am no longer the nymph I was.
(I've surpassed why, become because.)

This is the moment where I should
confess to feeling empty. Admit
I had it good as an ordinary bug,
reveal the loss of viscera made
me less than I had been, and flight,
which had been of me, is lost to the line's tug.
But I know better. In the water,
in their hunger, the fish gather.

And then the air which had been bright
is bright again, I flash through dapple,
come clean from blue shadow, vanish
and return, and the water is not flat —
it flirts, baits, is muscled with ripple,
one body and every body, and a fish
erupts from its living opacity.
The hook bites —
                              the line snaps —
                                        I'm free —

at last to curl and plunge and tumble
in the dark, through wrack and litter,
to love the blackness as it bears
me under. I'm sunk in silt, and still
the creek is rived with light; I glitter
in the black of strata, and the stars
of rotifers fall slowly to inter
my resin corps—Larkin's Blue Wonder.

Accept No Imitations

"Ce qui me semble, à moi, le plus haut dans
l'Art (et le plus difficile), ce n'est ni de faire
rire, ni de faire pleurer, ni de vous mettre en
rut ou en fureur, mais d'agir à la façon de la
nature, c'est-à-dire de faire rêver."
—Gustave Flaubert

I wake and everything is backwards.
Flossing is difficult, but the shower
pours full into my face,
which is a hell of a wake-up.
I spread the newspaper out
on the roughsawn table and sit backwards
in my chair: Tight End Injures Tailbone,
Future Uncertain; Fed Declares
Smurfit-Stone Superfund Site, Moss Gains
Baby Weight, something political
always and an ad for one of those
French waters: *Eviter Les Contrefaçons.*
Touching the print
I can no longer feel the depth
of the type set in the page;
or perhaps it is the paper,
no longer extrusive.
It is hard to feel like anything matters.

Philematology

Despite H1N1, airborne vectors
for terrorist threats, despite the flocked

wind carrying asbestos in the dust
of the building going down across the river,

despite the long latencies of modern
pesticides, and in the face even

of ordinary cold, which keeps the mountains
in snow while the river slips its upstream ice

down the main channel, in clots, under flocks
of confused ducks—a man and woman

stand close to the riprap slope, mouth
to mouth, as if practicing their CPR.

Her hair blows past his neck,
catching in the army stubble there,

and all around them poplars touch boles,
their sap thinning as it rises to new leaves.

It is the flow of them,
the study of lovely materials.

A Dispensation
from the Vows

for Andy, on the 50th anniversary
of leaving the brotherhood.

The wind is divisible
and currents break down to ghosts
ghosts to molecules, animalcules,

the countless generations of insects, illuminations
prior to embodiment. The wing of an elm seed
acts as a knife, to cut

some small collection from the whole
and spin it round, out over the road,
and up, and back, to ring the elm's trunk.

She is that seed, and you, brother,
that pocket of air, which did not know itself
until she curled around you, translucent.

Coyote Elegy

He's lickety-split frolic
and bombastic tricks; he struts,
walks tall, calls out catcalls
from the lucky black of his now human,
now inhuman throat; now
he's a huckster circa eighteen
sixty-six, a carpetbagger preaching
his virtuous elixirs nonpareil,
extracts of ragwort and thistle,
and various secret ingredients. Now
he's a dancer, and his feet flash
and the rickety platform cracks
with each footfall, now it's his wedding night
in this hemlock glade,
and the homemade champagne mills
in its dull bottles, and he is young,
again, and each time this night happens
it is his, he is a blur of shadow
littering the ground under the tree-figured
sky, he is Pan-god, goat-god, half-good
half-mad trickster, hear how his breathing
never slows, and his panting, his grunting
gives him away as a charlatan,
not one man only on this sole
impermanent night, but every man,
and the gap between this godhood
and that one lone man is a gulf so great
and wide the bright of his girl-wife
dims as she dances close, the strings
of her sandals creasing her calves, her hair
trailing her as she dances to him
unconcerned, and he stops

drinking, stops dancing
long enough to call out,
o god, o dear, don't—

go, he finishes, as the dark
closes over her, and he is lost
again into the unending whirlygig.

Travels in Requiem

1. *Introitus*

Snow slows the night down, unknowing,
unknown, burning orange under one
streetlight, blue-shifted at the next, each sphere
an oncoming or receding galaxy
lost in the star-thick dark.

2. *Sequentia*

Beside the small space of one light's universe
buried in a barrow-vault, the municipal turbines hum
with contained speed; under my feet water piped down
from the falls flows to light acres and arcs
of streets, great halls of train stations and factories,
warrens of houses and hospitals, all that net flow
shut in and running, first, smooth
through subterranean circumferences black and accurate, *dies irae,*
day of anger, *solvet saeculum,* dissolving the world, the vibration
moving up my feet, through my marionette back
and up on a high thread into the one lone dark
flocked with unseen snow, then
falling, no wind, and the trails of willows
fired in the city's night-red glow, the red of Paris intra-muros
rising over ranked berms, over the riverside transformer yard,
over catacombs filled with a pressure, cascade, descant,
water, thunder, a ghosted algal echo running
through the turbines' vanes, bright of the smallest
phosphorescences, protozoic borealis, sarcodinean
novae, sum of musics,
recordare, remember, *querens,* searching,
down through the catacombs
under the barrieres *d'Enfer,*
walking the ranked femurs

in the shallows of a greater fear, trailing a hand
over the socketed domes unthinking,
stopping to draw, in charcoal crosshatch, the eyes'
orbits, confusions. In the dark
of the cathedral after mass,
the pulse in my ears fills cells
superabundant with blood, courses over and amid
after-echo and ossicle, epithelial
transept, epithalamial crux, falls through arches
in the dark, flood of cooled stars, spires, flares:
June night at a field's verge in the Berkshires'
seas of fireflies, lightspill of my first flight descending
over New York, first night with a woman in Hawaii
in the mangoes in the rain, sparks spinning
over bonfires, cinders turning in the dark
and floating, falling, coming into being over streetlights
each now isolate and skewed from white
by the various longevities of filaments, *voca me
cum benedictus,* call me among the blessed.

3. Communio
Blued with height, the vault of Notre Dame du Haut
fills with the echoes of our voices, which descend,
a snow of sound, over our bodies singing.
It is late, the chaperones are all gone and we boys are lying, heads
together in a ring. This, my body, light
from its song, is a boy's body among the choir
of boys, and the echo, as it dies,
is of such clarity I'll know it all my life. *Lux
perpetua luceat,* let the light fall perpetual.

Singularity

There are seven billion of us now.
It is late summer and the flower fields
are gold with goldenrod, amaranth-red,
coded with pattern and pollen and the bloated
diode pods of butterfly weed. Without them
our long gestation would fail,
the worms of our untransformed forms
curl around their hunger, but summer
has been good to us and we
dry our wings in a sun-break
and lift into a sky lit
with the black and fire of us.

On the Way
to Catoctin

Morning comes up thick
in the grass and thatch
and sumac of the woods' verge,

carried up the way a bird
rides a thermal up,
over endless hills, phone lines,

and roads, over the heat map
of lives reclaimed from sleep,
rising into color, blanketing

the blue land in a mosaic
of reds, dense in grids
and looser elsewhere,

internal monologues spooling up
from dreams' halting
states, old arguments rehashed

in the space under
the shower's heat, separate
and brief and self-contained.

Unwaiting, the light continues
its plain growth, articulating
houses eaves and the certain

green of bracken uncoiling
into spring, over trees
ghosted with color, over the hills

various opacities, the verdigris
of lichens breaking down the mountains'
folds, and back into the clearing, into the drum

of my head beating, pulse thin
and lifting, getting up from the discomforts
of my bed, and getting going.

I don't know how many lives I passed
on the way to Catoctin,
there was rain and more

rain, I saw ground soft and green
with winter wheat, or broken
to rough crumble, a blurred

paintwork, canvas-coarse.
On the way to Catoctin, I looked
down new-laid asphalt-black

to future slums, fine vinyl townhomes
built four stories up, piebald
in partial brick, red hillsides

held in check with stacks
of concrete blocks, suppurating mud,
so much of all of this for sale,

so much foreclosed, so much arrayed
in palletized rows, ready
for the forklift-up, the truck-hoist-up

the rise of smoke from chimneys, steam
from valleys, the heron from the overgrown
retention pond past which the red roads

merge and flow, a sough of cars
from somewhere close to somewhere
else, each river-noise

muted and eased
into the rest. I knew
the world could not possibly be so large

as to offer such repetition,
and to require so much distance
for return; and yet it was,

and did, and I pulled
off for gas and closed my eyes,
my head usual and heavy.

Up ahead the fallow fields
and the harrowed fields lapped
against the rise of the earth's folds,

and there, without the highway's speed
and blur, the roads of my childhood
seemed about to appear, connecting

to the fragment I was on, standing by the car,
holding the pump full open and staring up
into the sky's straying

silver, steam rising from the coffee
in my other hand, motions unrandom
but unknowable, limned with the earth's ring.

Lost in Fireworks

Late on the Fourth of July I hear,
out in the dark somewhere, a kid crying.
There are two of them, each younger
than my own, one leading the other
down the street, through the trenches
of the sudden maples' shadows.

All night I listened to the scattered pop
and thud and throb, cascade of spark and crackle,
whistle, fusillade, ricochet. Each sound
drummed from the mountainsides, propagating,
splitting and converging, branching bright thickets,
night bats' sonar spread littering the cluster
and occlusion of the trees diffraction
gates, freshet of falling sparks settling from heat
to iron, the elements of suns' fusions belling out again
in their fixed procession, the casus-curve
of burning: hydrogen, lithium, sodium, potassium,
home? Not home yet home is somewhere some more houses down,

down through the cosmos of the too-large night,
in which I leave them, afraid to go out.

Listening for the Emperor of Ice Cream on a Rainy Afternoon

Why has the haft lost its rake? Whose boots
left the holes that are filling with rain?
And why is the garden a lake?
What is the talk that the rain overhears
running in place in the space of the drawn window sashes?
How long will this last?

What use is a hoe for a flight? What bird
doesn't cease on the chaise of the analyst?
And what about sight? Can vision be molecule-acute?
Or if, failing that, can it make out at least if it's chigger or tick
half-sunk in the skin on my older son's neck?
I've no tool for this—how long will it last?

Why listen for song to come carnival-cute?
Why buy him a treat? Why not make him wait?
Surely, if road is to weather as lactose to suck
then wishful's to waffle as laughter to lack?
Why else would the rain try to talk?
(How long can its muttering last?)

And what of the dieseling truck? Surely
there's somewhere to be? What semblance of hope
can an ape entertain, when stuttering
leads to the sea? When culture is careful
and artful and always one way?
What son wants to stay?

If hunger is sweet what does waiting abet?
And when will the sun come unsunk?
If we wait for the song

of the popsicle truck, with the greying soft
lock of the rain on the face of the garden,
what hurt is a burden?

I sit with my son, my son fidgeting; I wonder,
my heart in its halter of rain,
what is song? What is song?

Stopping by a Mint Field on the Eastside Highway

In the dry thatch of the road's verge
she stopped the car and waded out
into the field, the scent not catching up to her
at first, then overpowering, a mindless
cold and sweet and wet and mint.
She took the tire-iron from the trunk,
wanting to lay out some vast
crop circle-ish design. She swung,
the iron flattening the plants,
carving arcs, paisleys, mandlebrots,
and she was smiling, imagining
the farmer coming on some inscrutable alien
design. Hers.
High up now, she sculled the summer air
towards spring, her body thawing
from the furrowing of age. So light.
She saw the shadow of herself ragged
on the ruined crop, penumbra and straw,
her body lighter than linen, flaxen
in long sun, cells
fluxing. In the sudden cold
of a passing cloud she could feel mint oil
on the roof of her mouth, the chemo aftertaste.
The noise of cars
rose from the road, a flood first high
then low. The last of the sun
came fast across the field
and flushed her skin.
Always someone, she thought,
going. She laughed and lit up.

The Pleasures
of the Alphabet

1. Summer
It is mid-August, and the dust and fire-smoke
give way to rain, not for an afternoon,
but for two long otherworldly weeks:
verdant, English, biblical.

Out through the wide double doors
the rain lays the ash leaves flat,
the road is black, and clouds rise
from the ragged folds of mountainsides.

Even in the mountains the world sums
to flat; fields and fences
average out; the scrawl of rocks;
the phone lines gentle catenaries.

In all of this a woman laughs on her phone,
standing under a juniper, in the lines of rain.

2. Fall
Letters grow like fruit,
pendant and discrete; words
form without syntax, just color
or scent without context.

When vowels fall, they drop quick
striking the ground and rolling
among the incomprehensible blades of grass.
Still, sense remains, up in the branches.

When consonants split the whole tree shakes,
and creaks, and shoots curt clicks, the old wood
checks and the new wood breaks.
And then wind uncreates.

In the stream beside the tree
the letters rattle and collect.
Languages come to be and pass,
and there is something else, too small to see:

The dappled shadows move, coalesce
and disperse, a broken place, delayed
sky, makeshift gestalt, well-hid
half scented idea-of, dark shuttling

manifold signs—though thrown
by letters they almost seem alive,
and so believe themselves the cause
of whole unfallen sentences.

3. Winter
The streetlight holds a world of snow,
whole genus of pictographic script,
and though each flake participates in soundlessness
somehow the gist comes clear.

4. Spring
Vines on the porch swell at the bud-scar.
A ladybug crawling on the glass.
The pertinence of pleasing things
does not last.

In the dry garden
new snow creates a page
under old writing.